W9-AUY-423

Illustrated by
Karen McKee and Georgene Griffin

Published by Rourke Publishing LLC
Copyright © 2002 Kidsbooks, Inc.

Printed in the USA

Rourke Publishing LLC
Vero Beach, Florida 32964
rourkepublishing.com

McKee, Karen
Airplanes / Karen McKee and Georgene Griffin, ill.
p. cm – (How to draw)
ISBN 1-58952-151-X

INTRODUCTION

This book will show you how to draw lots of different, cool
planes with hot wings. Some are more difficult than others, but if you follow along,
step-by-step, you'll soon be able to draw many different aircraft.

SUPPLIES

NUMBER 2 PENCILS	FELT-TIP PEN
SOFT ERASER	COLORED PENCILS
DRAWING PAD	MARKERS OR CRAYONS

Each airplane in this book begins with several basic shapes—
usually a combination of ovals and triangles.
Many variations of these shapes, along with other lines, will also be used.

HELPFUL HINTS

1. In the first two steps of each drawing you will create a solid foundation of the figure (much like a builder who must first construct a foundation before building the rest of the house). Next comes the fun part—creating the smooth, clean outline of the winged aircraft and adding all the finishing touches, such as details, shading, and color.

Note: Following the first two steps carefully will make the final steps easier.

2. **Always keep your pencil lines light and soft.** These "guidelines" will be easier to erase when you no longer need them.

3. **Don't be afraid to erase.** It usually takes a lot of drawing and erasing before you will be satisfied with the way your drawing looks. Each image has special characteristics that make it easier or, in some cases, harder to draw. However, it is easier to draw anything if you first break it down into simple shapes.

4. Add details and all the finishing touches **after** you have blended and refined all the shapes and your drawing is complete.

5. **Remember:** Practice Makes Perfect. Don't be discouraged if you can't get the hang of it right away. Just keep drawing and erasing until you do.

HOW TO START

1. Begin by drawing the basic overlapping shapes, such as the ones in step #1 below, for the general outline of the plane. It's usually easier to begin by drawing the largest shape first. The dotted lines show what can be erased as you go along.

2. Sketch the other shapes **over** the first ones. These are the basic guidelines that create the foundation of your drawing.

Remember to keep your lines lightly drawn, and erase any guidelines you no longer need as you go along.

3. Carefully combine and blend all the lines and shapes to create the final outline. Once the aircraft

has a smooth, flowing look, begin adding the details that will make this hot-winged aircraft unique.

4. Continue to refine your drawing as you add all of the finishing touches. When your aircraft is complete, color it with your favorite colors or, for a more dramatic effect, outline it with a thick, black marker.

Use your **imagination** and feel free to create details other than the ones shown. You may even want to add backgrounds to enhance your drawings. When you have drawn some, or all, of the planes in this book and are comfortable with your drawing technique, start creating your own hot wings!

Most of all, HAVE FUN!

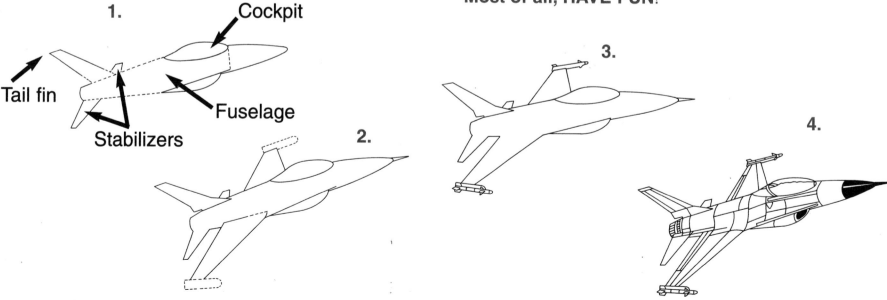

Grumman X-29

The forward wings of this experimental airplane enable it to be much more agile in flight.

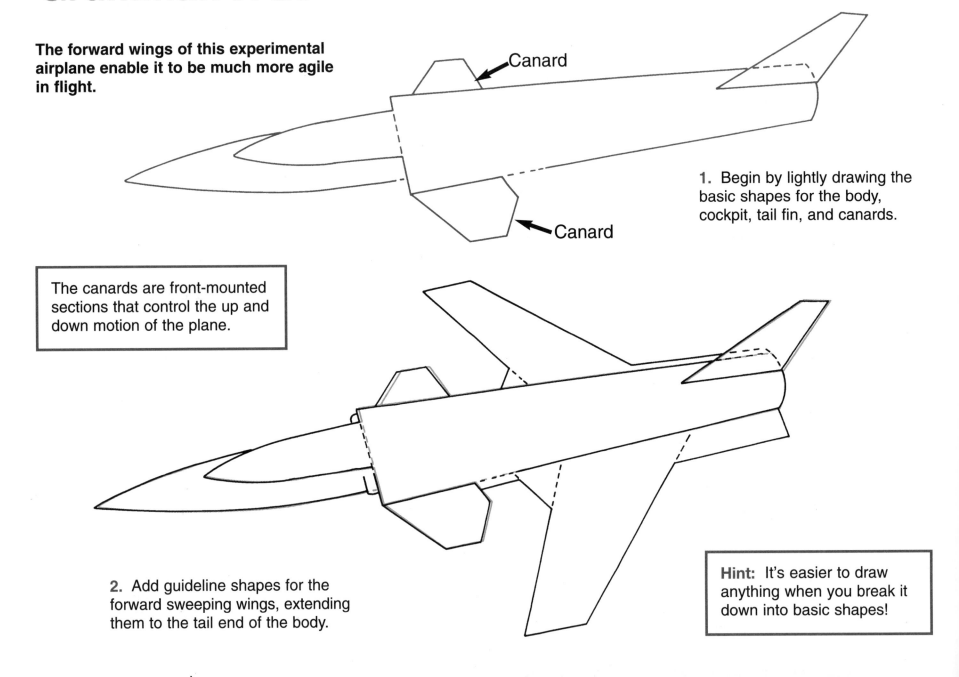

Canard

Canard

1. Begin by lightly drawing the basic shapes for the body, cockpit, tail fin, and canards.

The canards are front-mounted sections that control the up and down motion of the plane.

2. Add guideline shapes for the forward sweeping wings, extending them to the tail end of the body.

Hint: It's easier to draw anything when you break it down into basic shapes!

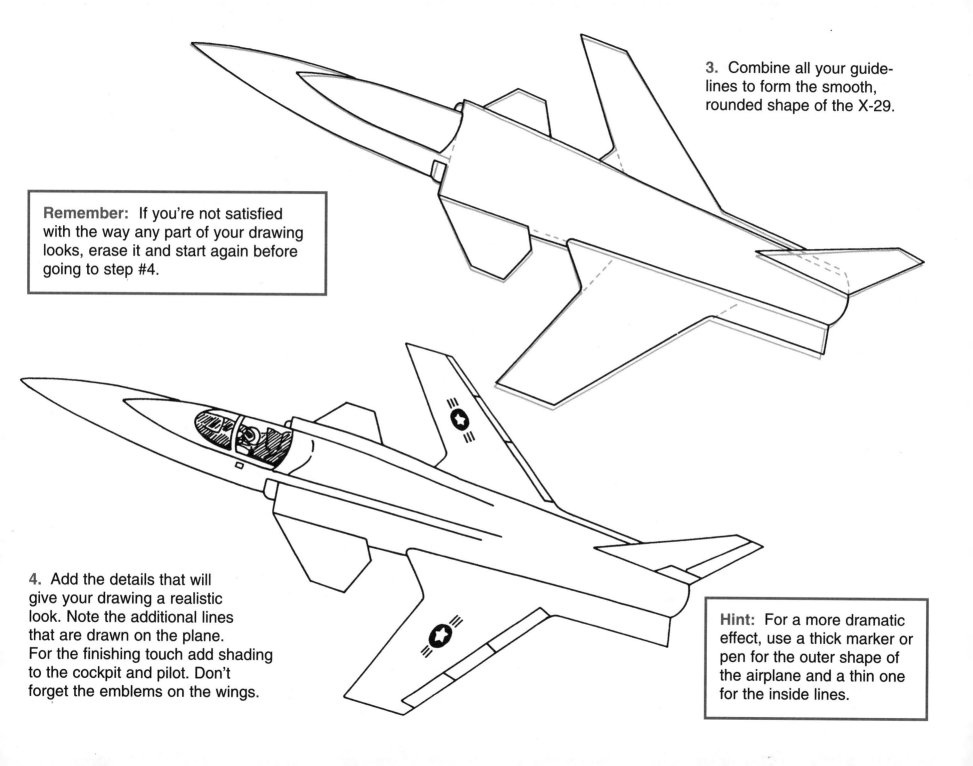

3. Combine all your guide-lines to form the smooth, rounded shape of the X-29.

Remember: If you're not satisfied with the way any part of your drawing looks, erase it and start again before going to step #4.

4. Add the details that will give your drawing a realistic look. Note the additional lines that are drawn on the plane. For the finishing touch add shading to the cockpit and pilot. Don't forget the emblems on the wings.

Hint: For a more dramatic effect, use a thick marker or pen for the outer shape of the airplane and a thin one for the inside lines.

Piper Archer II

The Piper Archer II is a four-seater, low wing, deluxe private plane.

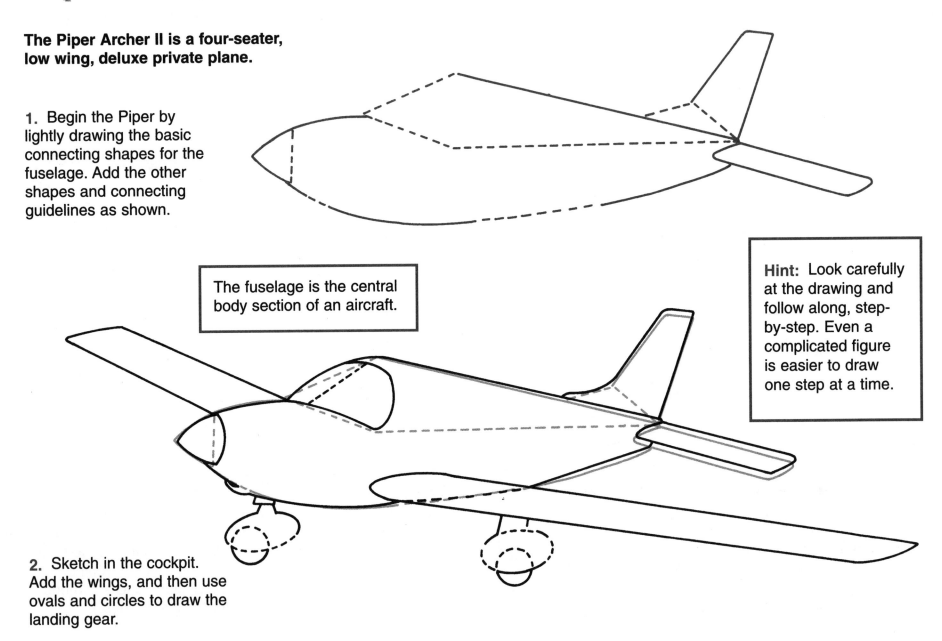

1. Begin the Piper by lightly drawing the basic connecting shapes for the fuselage. Add the other shapes and connecting guidelines as shown.

The fuselage is the central body section of an aircraft.

Hint: Look carefully at the drawing and follow along, step-by-step. Even a complicated figure is easier to draw one step at a time.

2. Sketch in the cockpit. Add the wings, and then use ovals and circles to draw the landing gear.

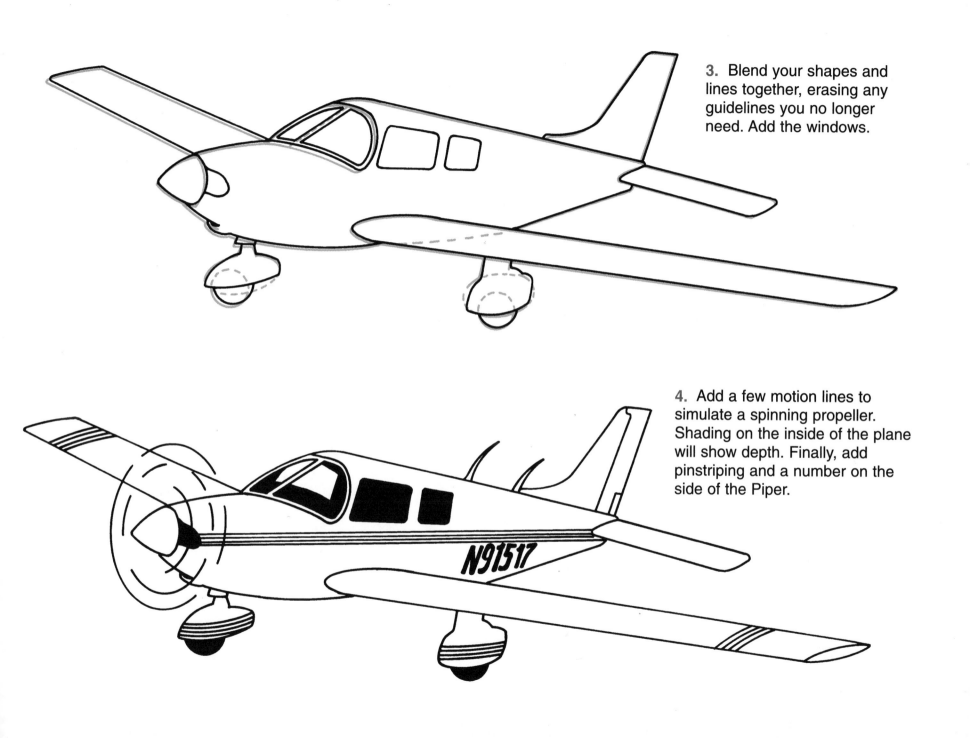

3. Blend your shapes and lines together, erasing any guidelines you no longer need. Add the windows.

4. Add a few motion lines to simulate a spinning propeller. Shading on the inside of the plane will show depth. Finally, add pinstriping and a number on the side of the Piper.

N91517

F-16 Fighting Falcon

The F-16 can be used as a fighter plane or as a light bomber.

1. Start your drawing by sketching basic shapes for the body, tail fin, and stabilizers. Try to get a rough feel for the overall shape of the aircraft. Don't be too concerned about details at this point.

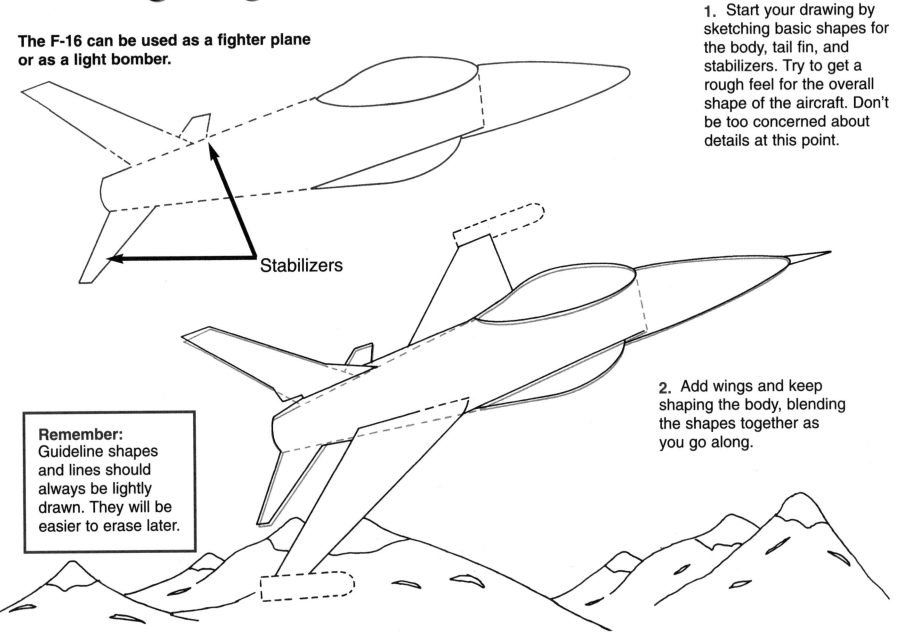

Stabilizers

2. Add wings and keep shaping the body, blending the shapes together as you go along.

Remember: Guideline shapes and lines should always be lightly drawn. They will be easier to erase later.

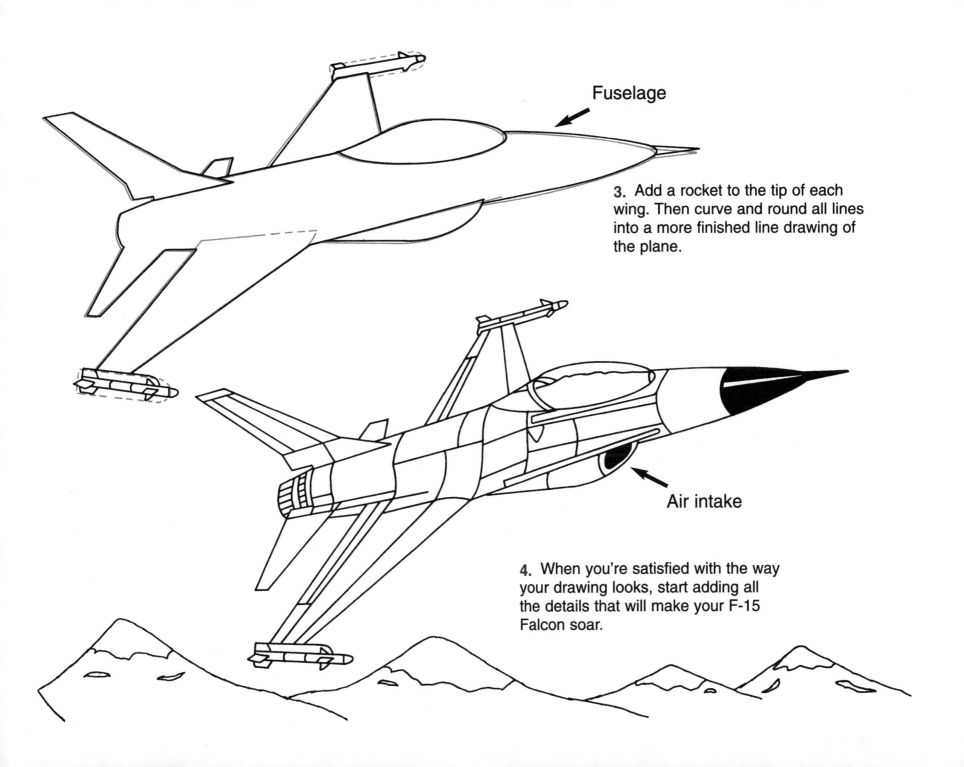

Fuselage

3. Add a rocket to the tip of each wing. Then curve and round all lines into a more finished line drawing of the plane.

Air intake

4. When you're satisfied with the way your drawing looks, start adding all the details that will make your F-15 Falcon soar.

Russian SU-27 Flanker

The Flanker is an all-weather fighter plane that can carry laser and TV-guided bombs.

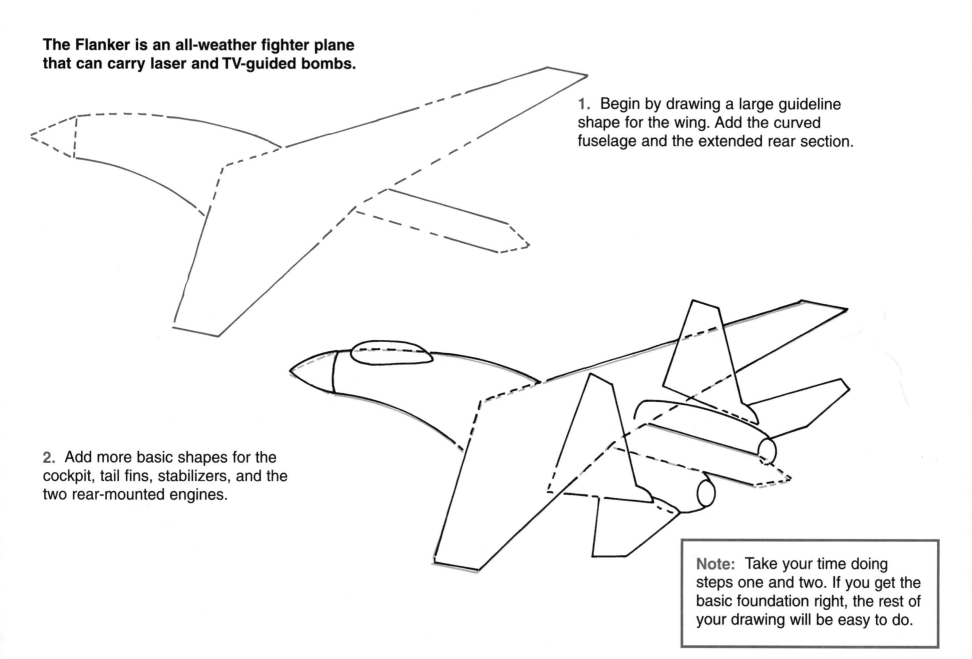

1. Begin by drawing a large guideline shape for the wing. Add the curved fuselage and the extended rear section.

2. Add more basic shapes for the cockpit, tail fins, stabilizers, and the two rear-mounted engines.

Note: Take your time doing steps one and two. If you get the basic foundation right, the rest of your drawing will be easy to do.

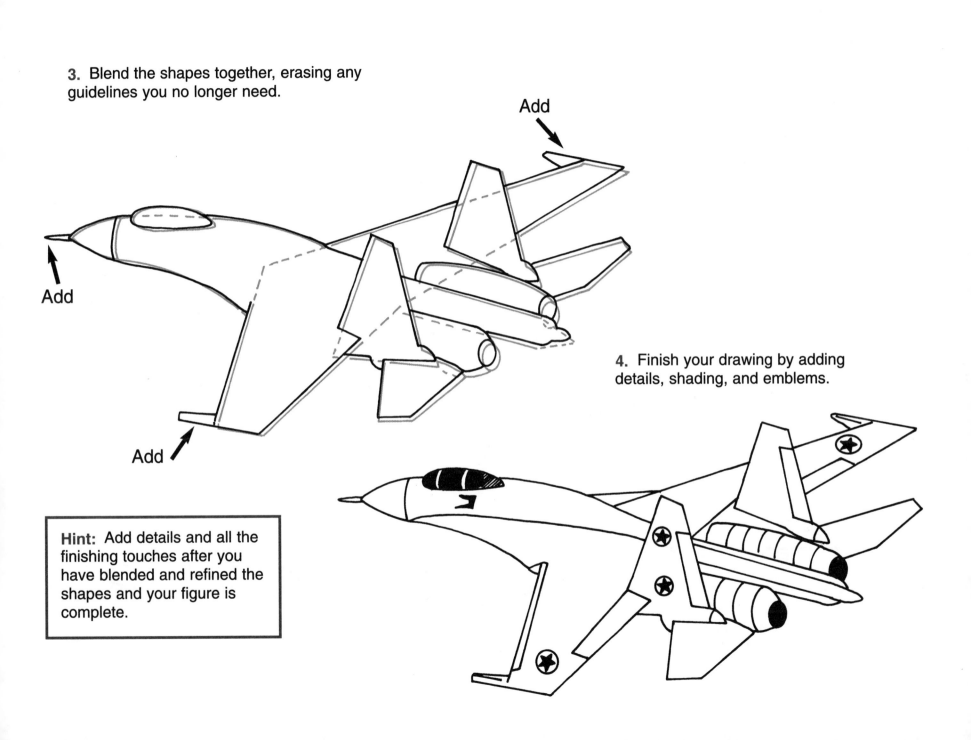

3. Blend the shapes together, erasing any guidelines you no longer need.

Add

Add

Add

4. Finish your drawing by adding details, shading, and emblems.

Hint: Add details and all the finishing touches after you have blended and refined the shapes and your figure is complete.

F-117 Stealth Fighter

Also known as the Night Hawk, this plane's "skin" absorbs radar waves, and its design scatters the waves, making the aircraft appear as a small bird on radar screens.

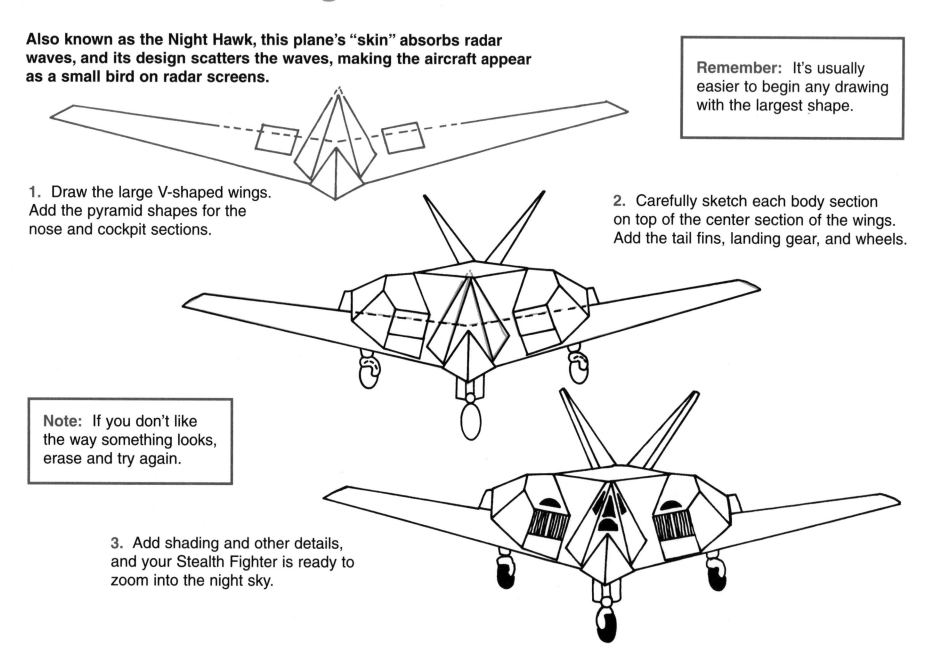

1. Draw the large V-shaped wings. Add the pyramid shapes for the nose and cockpit sections.

2. Carefully sketch each body section on top of the center section of the wings. Add the tail fins, landing gear, and wheels.

3. Add shading and other details, and your Stealth Fighter is ready to zoom into the night sky.

Long-EZ/XP

This sleek, home-built aircraft has a fiberglass/foam structure and weighs about 950 pounds.

1. Sketch a large, stretched-out football shape for the fuselage. Add the cockpit, canards, and a circle for the spinning propeller at the rear.

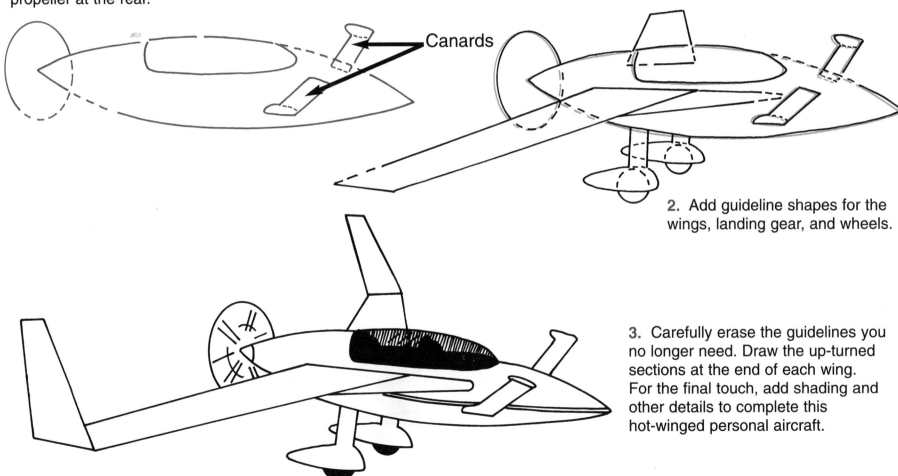

Canards

2. Add guideline shapes for the wings, landing gear, and wheels.

3. Carefully erase the guidelines you no longer need. Draw the up-turned sections at the end of each wing. For the final touch, add shading and other details to complete this hot-winged personal aircraft.

EFA Eurofighter

The Eurofighter was developed by several European countries. The front-mounted canards make it a very agile aircraft.

1. Begin your drawing by sketching basic shapes for the body, nose, cockpit, tail, and canard.

2. Add the triangular wings and the ovals beneath the wing and on the wing tips.

Remember: Take your time doing steps 1 and 2. If you get the basic foundation right, the rest of your drawing will be easy to do.

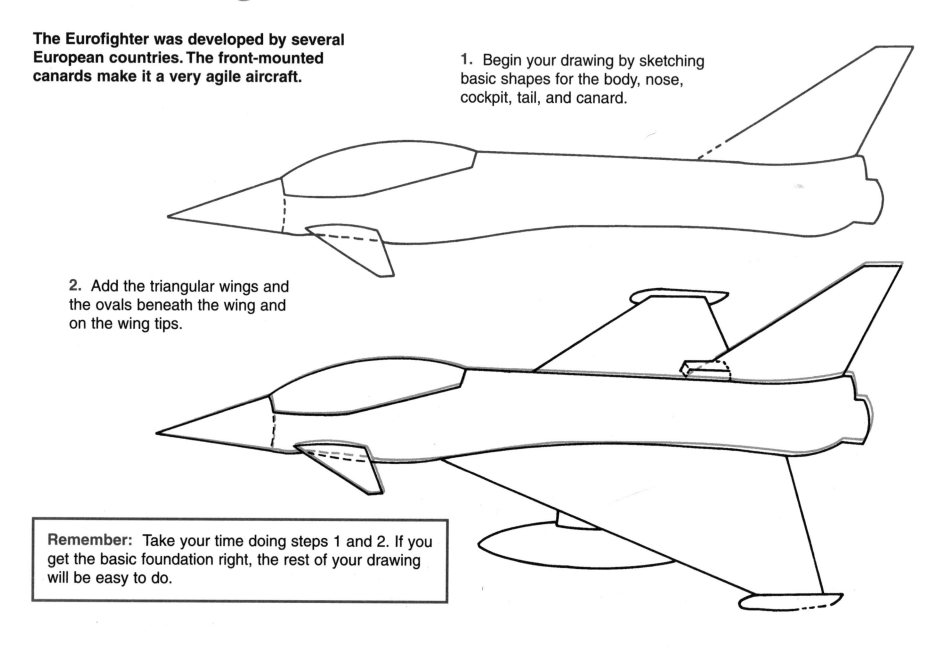

3. When all your guidelines have been drawn, blend them into a continuous body shape. Add the landing gear and erase any lines you no longer need

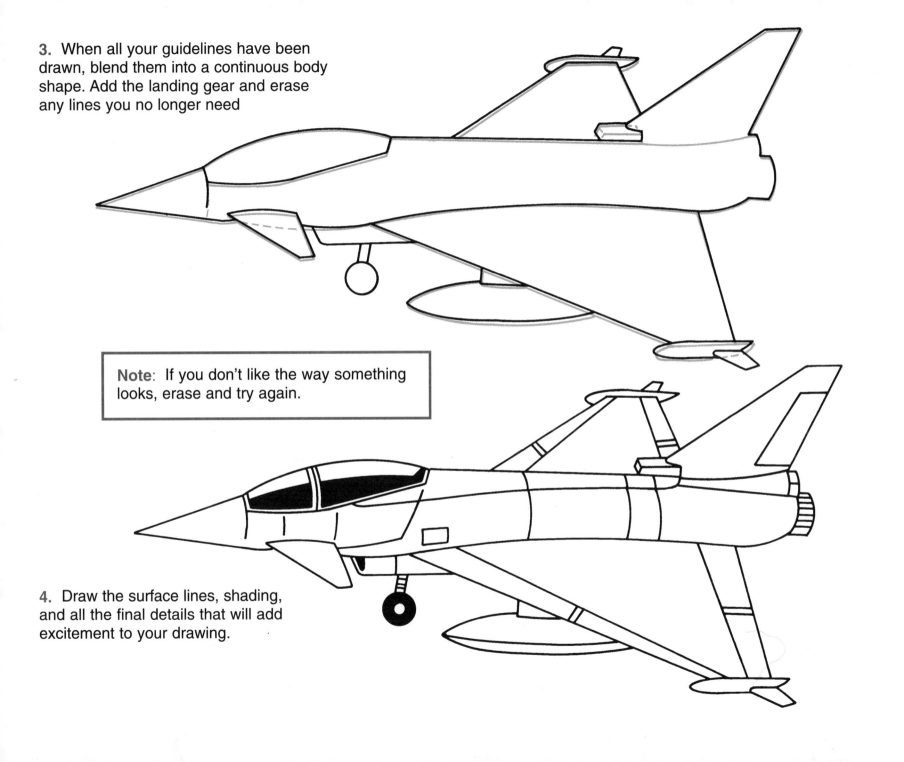

Note: If you don't like the way something looks, erase and try again.

4. Draw the surface lines, shading, and all the final details that will add excitement to your drawing.

Grumman E-2C Hawkeye

The Hawkeye may look difficult to draw, but if you follow along step-by-step, you'll have a fine, finished drawing.

This surveillance airplane has an advanced radar system mounted on top of its fuselage. The Hawkeye is capable of detecting other airborne craft hundreds of miles away.

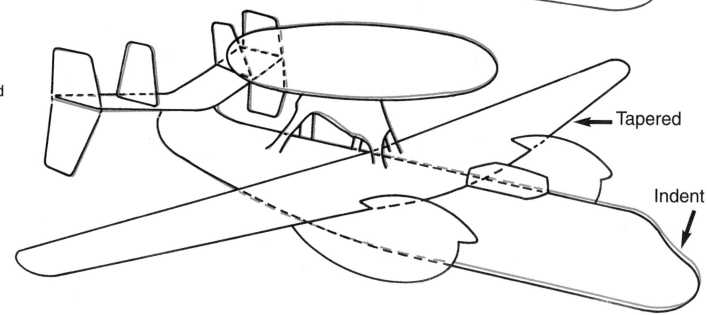

1. Begin by drawing a long oval for the body. Then add the other simple shapes for the tail section and radar system.

2. Add the single wing and guideline shapes for the engines. Note that due to the angle that the airplane is being veiwed, one end of the wing is tapered. In reality, both ends of the wing are the same.

Tapered

Indent

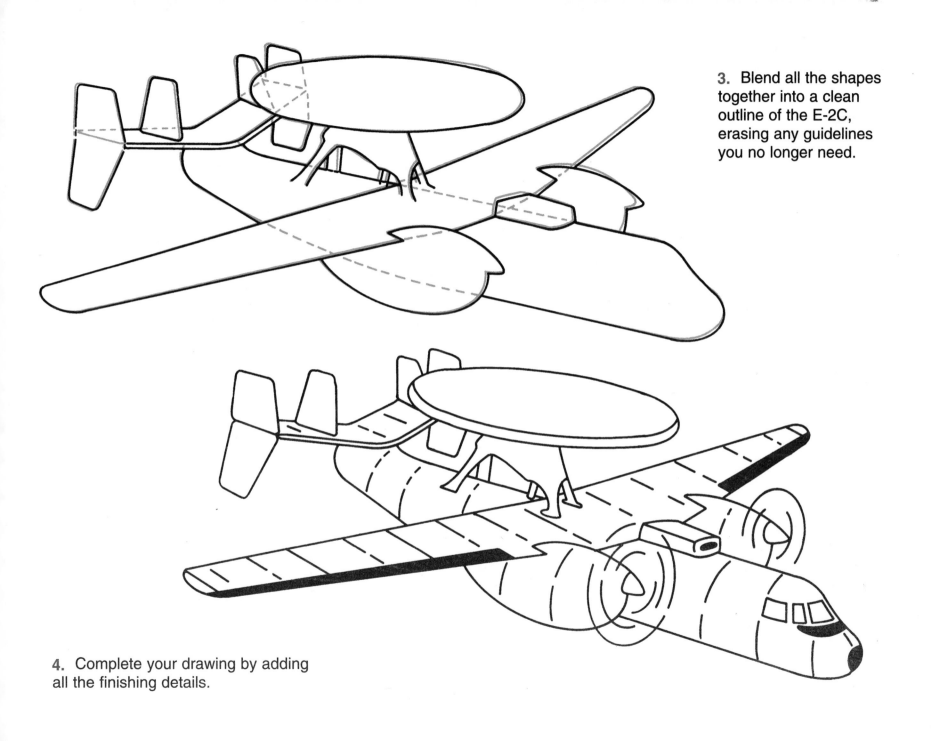

3. Blend all the shapes together into a clean outline of the E-2C, erasing any guidelines you no longer need.

4. Complete your drawing by adding all the finishing details.

Concorde

The Concorde is a supersonic commercial airplane that travels fast enough to break the sound barrier and high enough to see the Earth's curve.

Note: Always draw guide-lines lightly. If you don't like the way something looks, erase and try again.

1. Draw a long oval, pointed at both ends, for the body. Then add a large triangle for the wings.

2. At the bottom of each wing, add four small rectangular shapes.

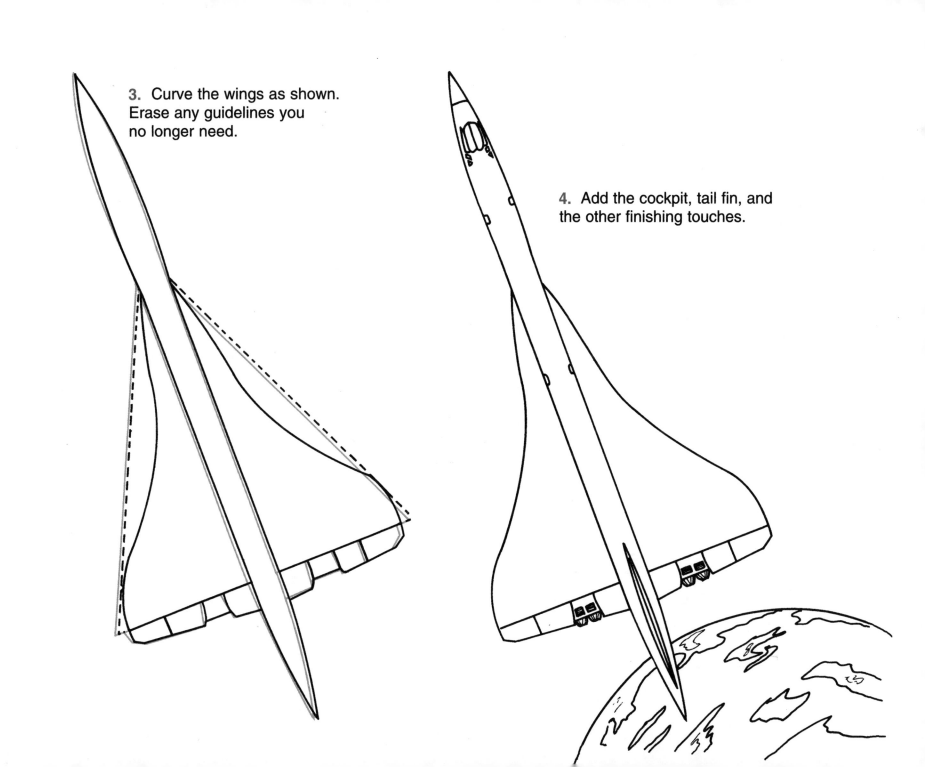

3. Curve the wings as shown. Erase any guidelines you no longer need.

4. Add the cockpit, tail fin, and the other finishing touches.

Hang Glider

A hang glider is powered only by the wind. The pilot's body is used to steer and control the craft.

1. Start by sketching a stretched-out diamond shape. The shape can be as large or as small as you like.

2. Next, lightly draw in the glider supports and cross bar.

Cross bar

Supports

3. Finish your drawing by adding the pilot, cords, and triangular steering bar. Then add your own design and colors to your glider.

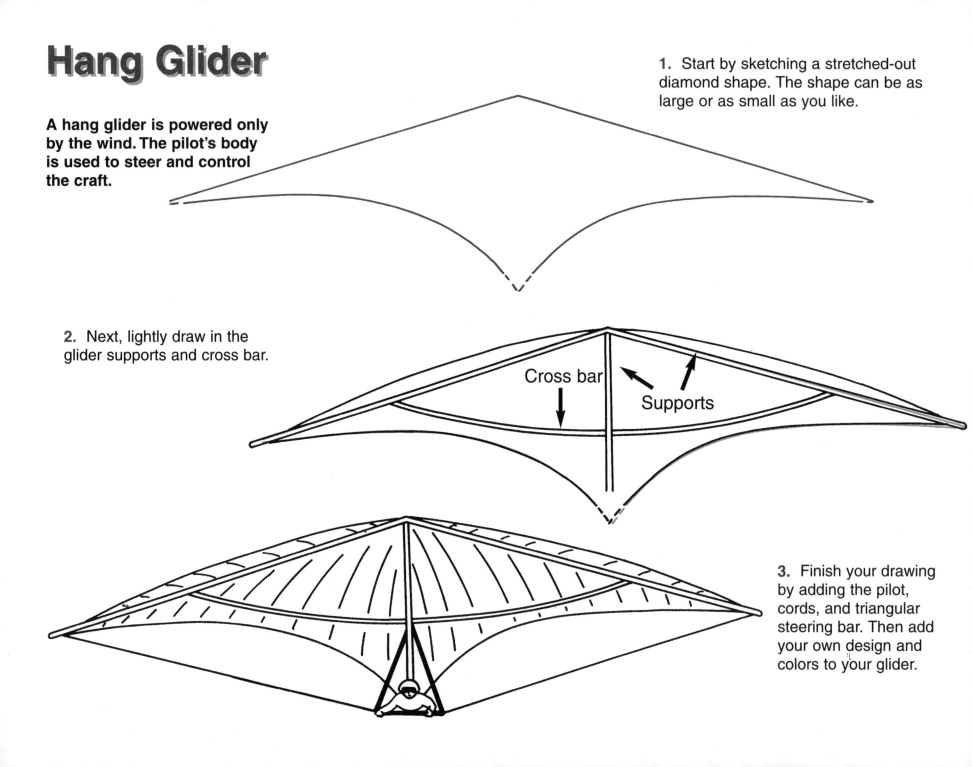

F-22 Raptor

The new Raptor is expected to become the world's dominant air superiority fighter plane.

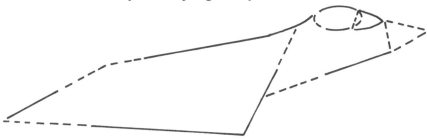

1. Begin by lightly drawing the large, flat wing section. Add the fuselage, cockpit, and nose.

> **Remember:** Practice makes perfect. Keep drawing and erasing until you are satisfied with the way your picture looks.

2. Add the triangular tail fins and the rear stabilizers. Begin defining and refining each section of the plane.

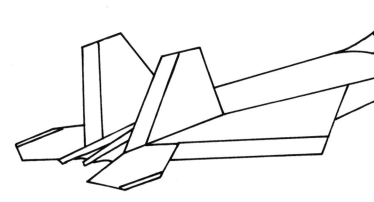

3. Complete the tail fins. Then blend the shapes and lines together. Finish the Raptor by shading the cockpit and adding the nose point.

FB-111

Known as the "Aardvark" because of its long, droopy, radar-filled snout.

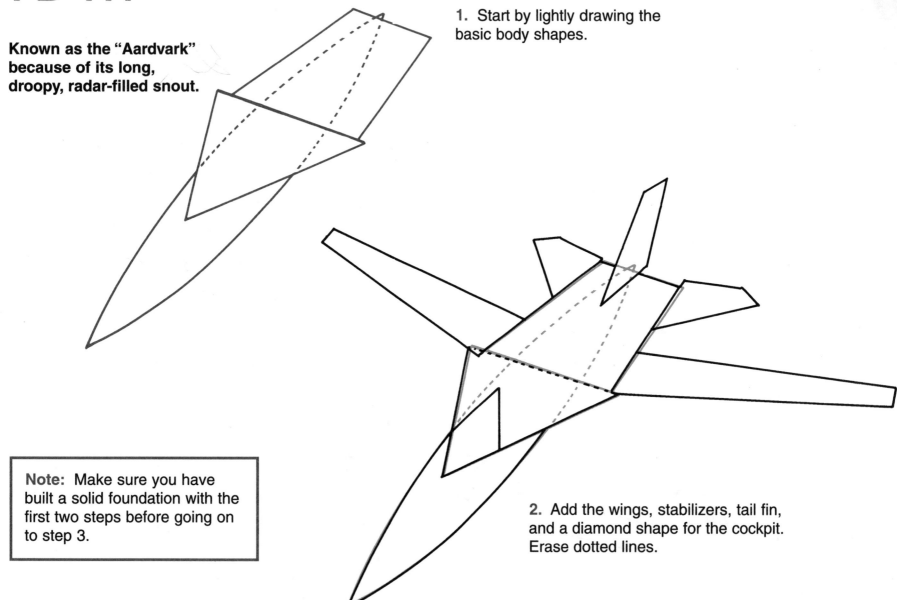

1. Start by lightly drawing the basic body shapes.

Note: Make sure you have built a solid foundation with the first two steps before going on to step 3.

2. Add the wings, stabilizers, tail fin, and a diamond shape for the cockpit. Erase dotted lines.

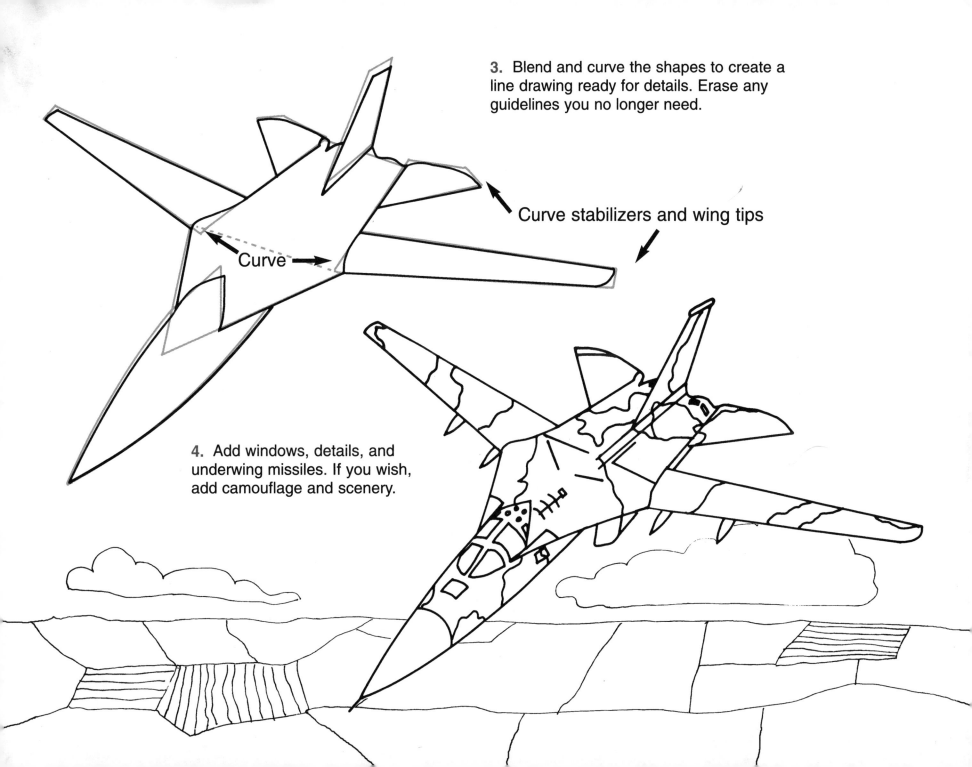

3. Blend and curve the shapes to create a line drawing ready for details. Erase any guidelines you no longer need.

Curve stabilizers and wing tips

Curve

4. Add windows, details, and underwing missiles. If you wish, add camouflage and scenery.

V-22 Osprey

The Osprey takes off like a helicopter and flies like an airplane.

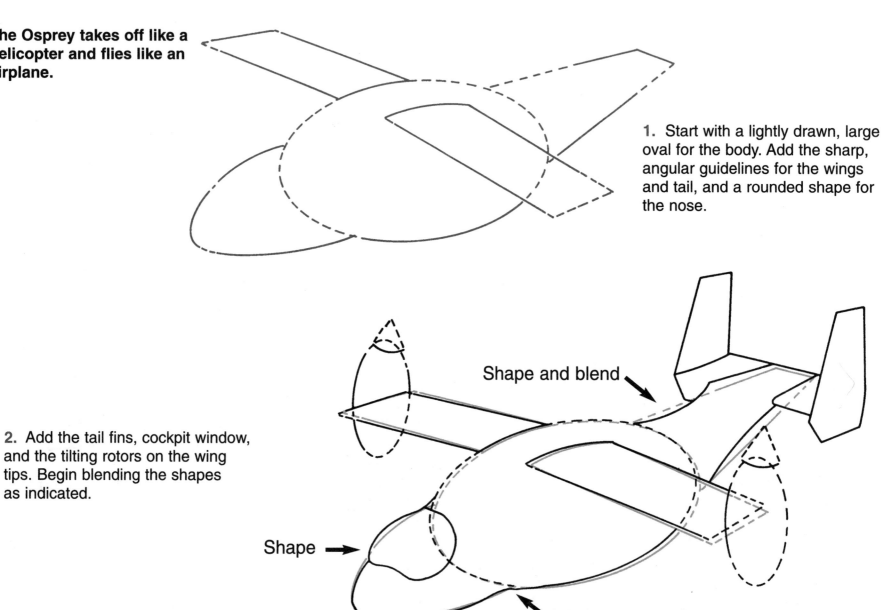

1. Start with a lightly drawn, large oval for the body. Add the sharp, angular guidelines for the wings and tail, and a rounded shape for the nose.

2. Add the tail fins, cockpit window, and the tilting rotors on the wing tips. Begin blending the shapes as indicated.

Shape and blend

Shape

Shape and blend

3. Combine the shapes into one smooth outline form. Keep erasing and drawing until your lines are just right.

The Osprey's rotors, on the end of each wing, can be tilted forward. This allows the craft to fly straight up like a helicopter or forward like a conventional airplane.

4. Now add all the finishing touches—windows, lines, and other details. Don't forget the motion lines to simulate the fast-spinning rotor blades.

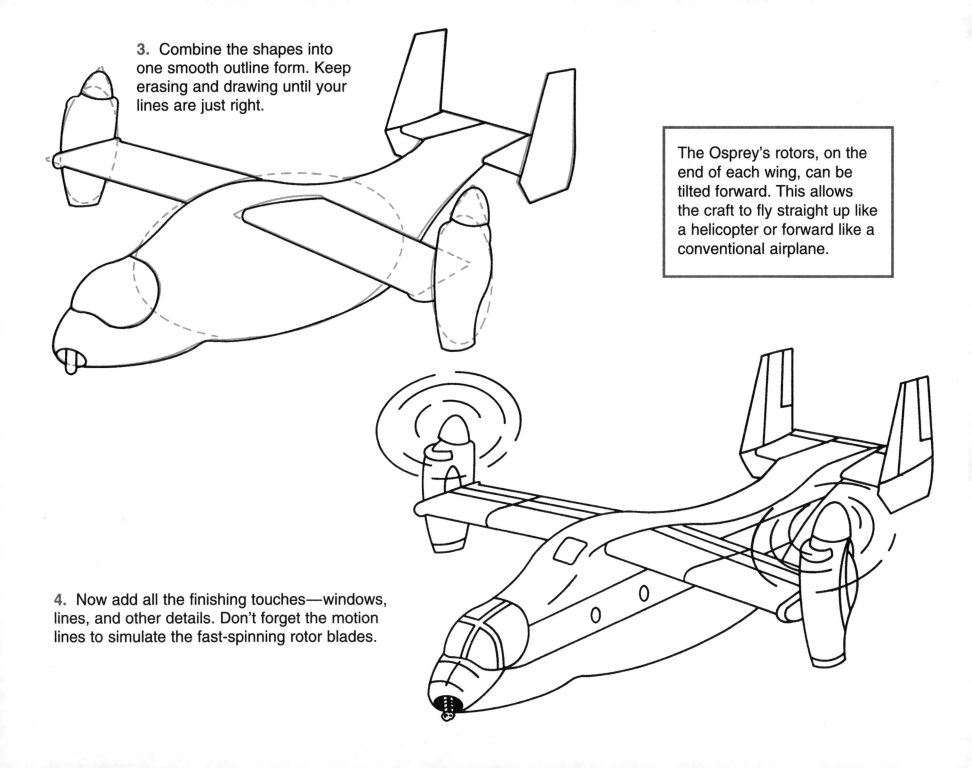

Stealth Bomber

Due to its unique "boomerang" shape and its ability to fly slowly at low altitudes, it is almost impossible for radar to detect the Stealth Bomber.

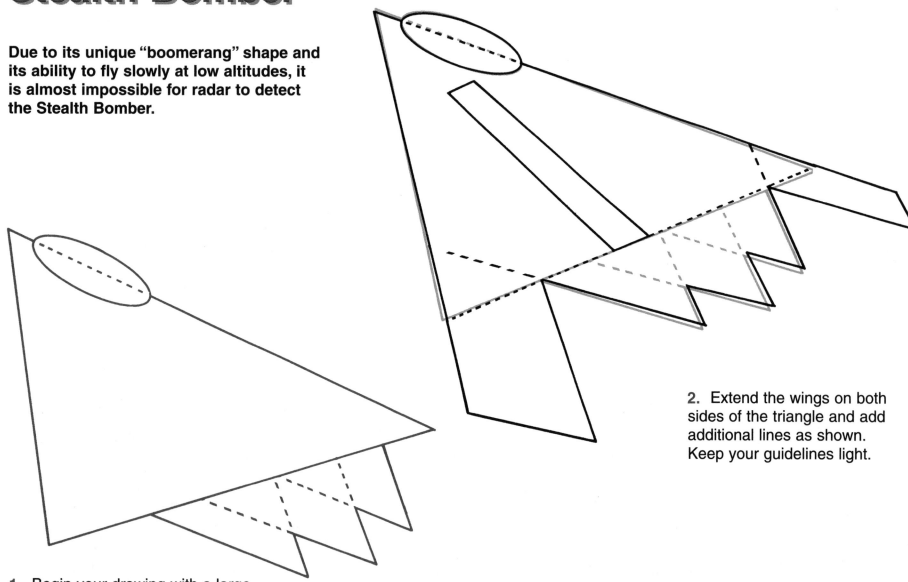

1. Begin your drawing with a large triangle. Add three small triangles on the bottom and an oval on top.

2. Extend the wings on both sides of the triangle and add additional lines as shown. Keep your guidelines light.

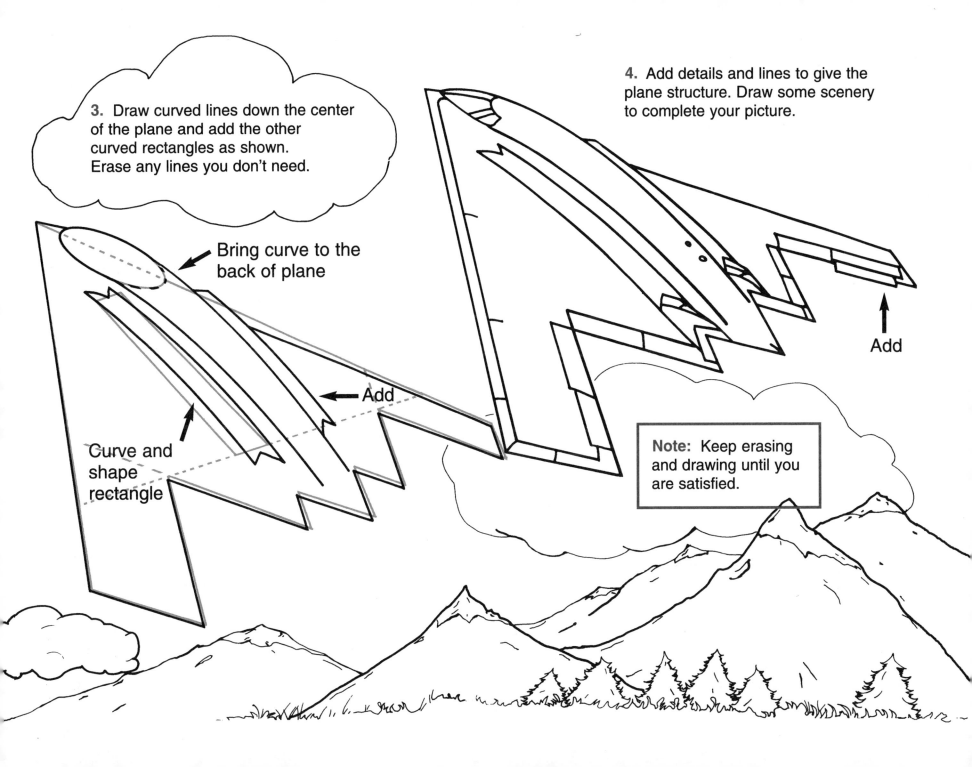

Russian S-37 Berkut

The forward-swept wings of the "Golden Eagle" fighter plane increase its maneuverability at high altitudes.

1. Begin by lightly sketching a rectangle for the Berkut's long body. Then add the simple shapes for the nose, cockpit, canard, and tail fins.

Remember:
Always draw your guidelines lightly in steps 1 and 2. It will be easier to erase them later.

Canard

Curve

Curve

Add

2. Carefully draw the wings, tail-mounted engine sections, landing gear, and wheels. Add the second canard and other shapes as shown. Curve parts of the plane as indicated, erasing any guidelines you no longer need.

3. Add the nose point and landing gear details. Then blend and refine all the lines and shapes into a smooth outline of the aircraft.

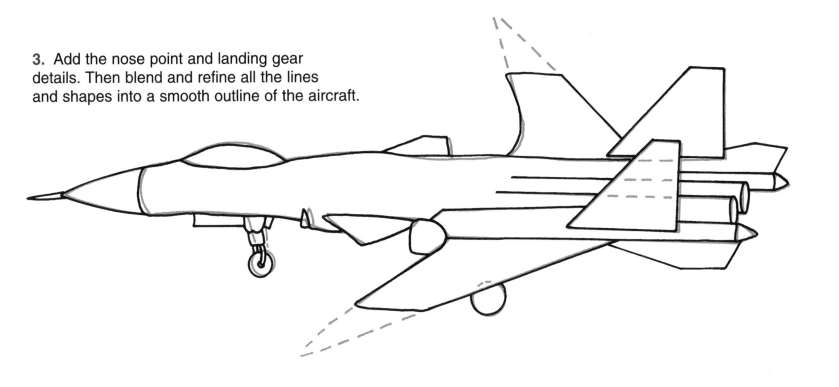

4. Complete your drawing by adding shading, body lines, insignia, and other details.

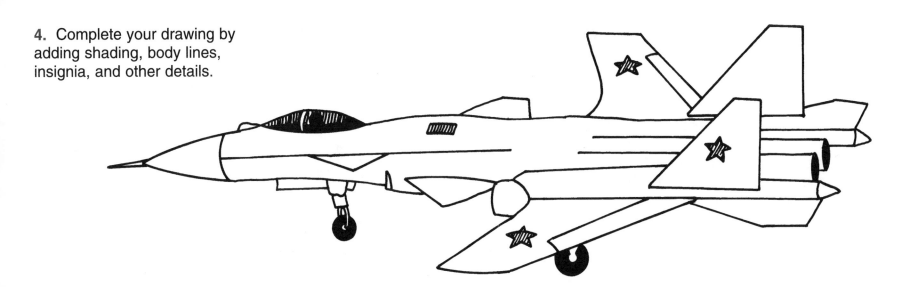

Aventura

The Aventura is a home-built seaplane that stands six feet high at wing level and can cruise at 75 miles per hour.

1. Start with a lightly drawn guideline shape for the large, single wing. Add the front and tail sections.

2. Draw guidelines for the large cockpit window, wing-mounted engine, and the pontoons (they allow the plane to land on water) under both sides of the wing. Add the stabilizers to the tail fin and a small circle on the side of the fuselage for the wheel.

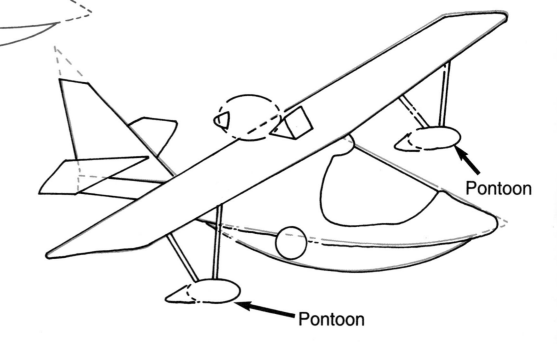

Pontoon

Pontoon

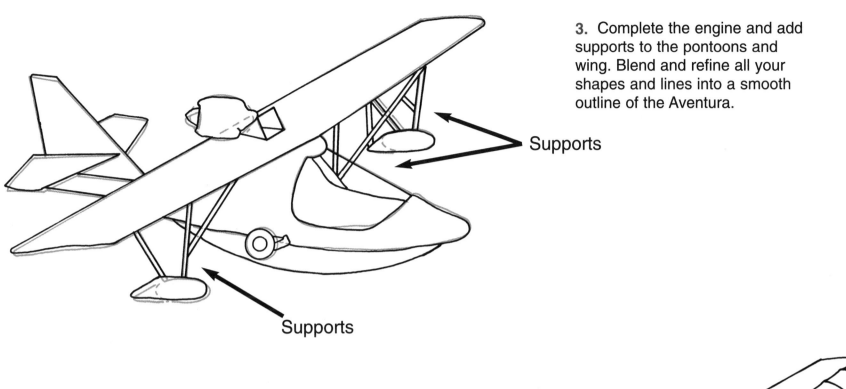

3. Complete the engine and add supports to the pontoons and wing. Blend and refine all your shapes and lines into a smooth outline of the Aventura.

Supports

Supports

4. Draw contours along the front edge of the wing, and add supports to the tail section. Add a spinning propeller, and complete the wheel. For the finishing touch, add two figures in the cockpit.

AV-8 Harrier

The Harrier's main mission is to provide close air support for the U.S. Marine Corps.

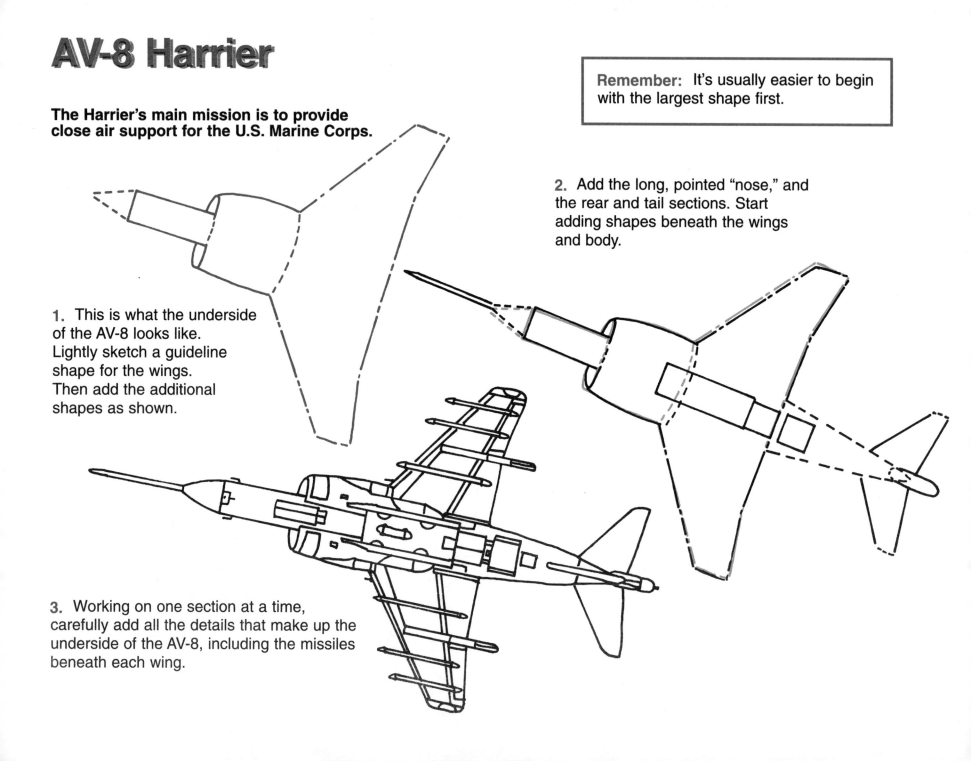

Remember: It's usually easier to begin with the largest shape first.

1. This is what the underside of the AV-8 looks like. Lightly sketch a guideline shape for the wings. Then add the additional shapes as shown.

2. Add the long, pointed "nose," and the rear and tail sections. Start adding shapes beneath the wings and body.

3. Working on one section at a time, carefully add all the details that make up the underside of the AV-8, including the missiles beneath each wing.